HAL LEONARD RHYTHM AND COUNTING

The Practical Handbook for Mastering Rhythm

BY DAVID HARRISON

PLAYBACK+
Speed • Pitch • Balance • Loop

To access audio visit:
www.halleonard.com/mylibrary
Enter Code
6776-6804-0384-5510

ISBN 978-1-70510-328-9

Visit Hal Leonard Online at
www.halleonard.com

Contact us:
Hal Leonard
7777 West Bluemound Road
Milwaukee, WI 53213
Email: info@halleonard.com

In Europe, contact:
Hal Leonard Europe Limited
42 Wigmore Street
Marylebone, London, W1U 2RN
Email: info@halleonardeurope.com

In Australia, contact:
Hal Leonard Australia Pty. Ltd.
4 Lentara Court
Cheltenham, Victoria, 3192 Australia
Email: info@halleonard.com.au

CONTENTS

INTRODUCTION

Welcome to *Hal Leonard Rhythm and Counting*. Of all the elements of music, rhythm is probably the most fundamental. Almost anyone can dance or clap along to a simple beat without any special musical training. But a proper understanding of rhythm is essential for all musicians at any level and any age. When it comes to studying rhythm, you'll soon encounter challenges, whether it's reading and writing rhythms correctly, understanding time signatures, or clapping and playing rhythms precisely.

This book is designed to take you through the fundamentals of reading and understanding rhythm in a systematic and practical way. You'll learn about basic concepts such as the beat, before being guided through simple rhythm symbols, rests, note groupings, time signatures, and all the other components of rhythm you're likely to encounter when playing music on any instrument. Towards the end of the book, you'll see some more advanced aspects, such as triplets, syncopation, and very short notes. This is a practical handbook. On every page there is an opportunity for you to practice counting and clapping rhythms, and each chapter concludes with a set of exercises for you to work through.

Take your time with these exercises and practice diligently, regularly varying the tempo you are working at. Eventually, you'll recognize the characteristic rhythms of common groupings, making reading and playing more intuitive. And be precise. Having a keen sense of the beat—that is, being able to play right on the beat—will elevate your music-making, especially when it comes to playing with other people.

Whatever your instrument, *Hal Leonard Rhythm and Counting* is your essential, practical handbook to mastering rhythm.

HOW TO USE THE AUDIO

Almost every musical example in this book is accompanied by play-along audio. The audio tracks also include several metronome clicks—beats at different speeds for rigorous, personal practice. Where the examples have four beats per measure (4/4, 4/2, 12/8, etc.) there is one measure of clicks. For all other time signatures, there are two whole measures of clicks. The exercises at the end of each chapter all carry a metronome marking to give you the tempo. Having different tempos will help you to develop a better understanding of rhythmic groups and the relationship bewteen various note symbols. At the end of this book, you'll find some bonus tracks; short pieces of music composed by the author to give you an idea of what music in various time signatures might sound like.

To access the accompanying audio, simply look for the 🔊 icon, go to www.halleonard.com/mylibrary, and enter the code found on page 1 of this book. This will grant you instant access to every file. You can download to your computer, tablet, or phone, or stream the audio live—and if your device has Flash, you can also use our PLAYBACK+ multi-functional audio player to slow down or speed up the tempo or set loop points. This feature is available exclusively from Hal Leonard and is included with the price of this book!

Thank you for choosing this book and good luck on your musical journey.

David Harrison

🔊 **Welcome to Hal Leonard Rhythm and Counting**

CHAPTER 1:
CONCEPTS IN RHYTHM

The Beat

Pretty much all the music we play has a beat to it. If you can count along to a regular pulse while the music's playing, you're hearing the beat. Dance music always has a good strong beat that's easy to hear and move to. Listen to a piece of music. Clap to the pulse. This is the beat.

Tempo

The speed of a beat is measured in *beats per minute* or *bpm*. Disco music, for example, has a speed of around 120 bpm, which is two beats a second. If you listen to a classic disco track, you'll hear the bass drum thudding constantly at about that speed.

The proper word for the speed of a piece of music is *tempo*. You might say things like, "be careful not to let the tempo drag," or maybe, "this is an unusually slow tempo," or even, "what tempo do you normally play this at?"

In classical music, there are other terms used to describe tempo, often in Italian. For now, we'll stick to bpm. If you use a metronome, the bpm is the setting that really counts.

Notation Basics

Rhythm is notated using various symbols. There are symbols to tell you when a note is played, how long it's played for, and how long to count before the next note is sounded. Then, there are symbols that tell you to play notes close together or to stop playing completely for a moment. There are even symbols asking you to play in a certain way.

Let's look at the way these symbols are set out. First, we need a set of horizontal lines, like a grid. Almost all instruments use this set of lines, which is called the *staff* or *stave*. Here's a completely empty staff.

All the symbols we use to show rhythmic information are placed along this staff, which runs from left to right. Let's place some notes on the staff. Here's a symbol that's often used to show a note that lasts a single beat, called a *quarter note*.

And here are several of these quarter notes, placed on the staff one after the other.

These notes are all on the middle line of the staff. The vertical placement of a note on the staff determines the *pitch* of the note (how high or low it sounds).

Since this book is only concerned with rhythm, we'll stick to using the middle line.

Bar Lines

Music is almost always divided up into units of time that group beats together. In this example, we've divided beats into groups of four by inserting horizontal lines after every four beats. These segments are known as *measures* and the dividing lines are called *bar lines*. Organizing rhythm in this way makes it much easier for musicians to read music accurately.

Often, you count with a special emphasis on the first beat. For example, you might count, "**one**-two-three-four, **one**-two-three-four," and so on as you follow the beats. Try clapping along with the quarter notes shown below, paying attention to the *beat count* written beneath them. You'll hear four quarter-note metronome clicks, followed by four measures of quarter notes. Focus on timing with nice even beats, and say the beat count out loud as you clap.

Notice the *metronome marking* at the beginning, indicating that the music contains 100 quarter-note beats in a minute.

Example 1

 Audio 01-01

Strong Beats and Weak Beats

As you count through these beats arranged in groups of four, you'll naturally *accent* (emphasize or stress) the first beat of the measure. An orchestral conductor might bring the baton down to show the first beat of the measure, and this beat is commonly known as the *downbeat*. The beat before this—the final beat of the previous measure—is called the *upbeat*. You might talk about the, "upbeat to measure three," for example. Or you might say, "that chord needs to be right on the downbeat."

There's another way to refer to beats in a measure that are naturally emphasized. Try counting in four and, aside from the first beat of each measure being accented, you will probably create a little accent on the third beat, too. With four beats per measure, the first and third beats are said to be *strong beats*, while the second and fourth beats are *weak beats*.

Listen to the audio example below to hear the difference in emphasis between various beats.

Example 2

 Audio 01-02

With a metronome track—or a metronome set to a moderate tempo—try clapping along to the beats in groups of four. Make the claps accurate and even, emphasizing the downbeat. You'll naturally make the upbeat that comes before it a little lighter in comparison. The second and third beats will likewise have a different emphasis, creating this sense of strong and weak beats. Try to feel the four beats working together to create a rhythmic pulse that revolves around the downbeat.

Percussion Clef

All the music in this book is written for rhythm instruments—and you can play the rhythms using any single note you like on a melody instrument such as a guitar, flute, or piano. Alternatively, you can sing them or play them on a percussion instrument. To indicate that notes have no melodic value, we use a special symbol called a *neutral clef* or *percussion clef*. All our exercises will begin with this symbol.

Double Bar Lines

One last thing. Music is often organized into sections such as an intro, verse, and chorus. To show when a section ends, we use a special kind of bar line called the *double bar line*. All our notation examples will finish with a double bar line from now on.

We've looked at the staff, measures, bar lines, and basic types of beats. In the next chapter, we'll look at more symbols and give them some names.

CHAPTER 2:
BASIC NOTE DURATIONS

The *duration* of a note (how long a note lasts compared to the length of a beat) is shown with the following symbols. These are known as *note values*.

The symbol that's used most often to represent a single beat is the one that we've already seen. It has a black *notehead* (the oval part) and a tail called a *stem*.

Basic Symbols

This is known as a *quarter note*. With four beats per measure, we'll have four quarter notes.

Quarter Note

For a note that lasts twice as long, the notehead is hollow. This note is called a *half note*. It is worth two quarter notes.

Half Note

To show a note that lasts for four beats, the symbol you'll need is a stemless, hollow notehead. This is called a *whole note*.

Whole Note

The whole note is the longest duration you'll commonly see. With four beats per measure, this symbol fills the whole measure.

Listen to the audio track and clap on the first beat of each measure. Hear how the note lasts right up to the end of the measure and be sure to say the beat count out loud as you clap. As before, you'll hear a measure of quarter-note clicks before the music begins.

Example 1

 Audio 02-01

Let's recap. A whole note is worth two half notes or four quarter notes. Listen to the audio track and count along, being sure to clap whenever a new note occurs in the music below. There will be a measure of quarter-note clicks before the music starts.

Example 2

Time Signatures

At the beginning of a piece of music, you'll always see a pair of numbers, one above the other. This pair of numbers is known as a *time signature*. The time signature determines the *meter*, which is the basic grouping of beats in a piece of music. It does this by providing two important pieces of information.

- Firstly, it tells you what sort of note value is used to show a single beat. We've already seen quarter-note beats in groups of four, so let's look at the way that is written. We use a "4" to signify a quarter note. This number is written below, like so.

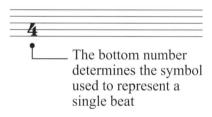

The bottom number determines the symbol used to represent a single beat

- Secondly, it tells you how many beats there are in each measure. In this case, the "4" on top indicates that we have four beats per measure.

The top number represents the beat counts per measure

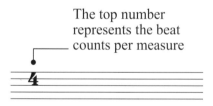

When you see this particular time signature, you'll know that you have four quarter-note beats per measure. It's referred to as "four-four"—also written as 4/4—and it's the most common time signature there is. If you play rock and pop, you will rarely come across a different time signature. In other kinds of music, such as folk, it's one of several time signatures you're likely to see.

4/4 is also known as *common time*. You'll sometimes see 4/4 written with a symbol that looks like a letter C instead of the numbers, like this.

Exercises

Now that we've got our 4/4 time signature, we can combine the symbols we've just encountered to create rhythms. In the following exercises, all the beats in each measure always add up to a total of four. Get used to counting, "one-two-three-four" along with the beats in 4/4.

You'll notice that the exercises have different metronome markings. If you're clapping along to the audio tracks, there will be a measure of quarter-note clicks before each exercise begins, which will give you time to get a feel for the tempo.

Take care, because some tempos are much faster than others! As you count, emphasize the strong beats, so you always know which beat is which.

 Audio 02-ex-01 to 02-ex-07

1. ♩ = 100

1   2   3   4   1   2   3   4   1   2   3   4   1   2   3   4

2. ♩ = 120

3. ♩ = 80

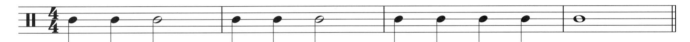

4. ♩ = 100

5. ♩ = 60

6. ♩ = 100

7. ♩ = 140

CHAPTER 3:
REST SYMBOLS

Now that we've had a look at some of the principal note symbols to show different durations, it's time to introduce the equivalent *rest* symbols. These are used to show that there's a silence in the music of a given length.

Here are the three symbols we've already seen with their equivalent rests.

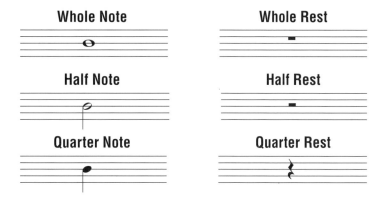

Notice that the whole rest and half rest look very similar. The half rest sits on the middle line, while the whole rest "hangs" from the line above. You'll almost always be able to tell them apart instantly from the context. In 4/4, if you've got any other notes in the measure, it'll have to be a half rest.

Here are quarter-note beats alternating with quarter rests. This means that there are notes on beats 1 and 3, with silence on beats 2 and 4. As you clap, say the beat count out loud.

Example 1

 Audio 03-01

A half rest is used to show two beats'-worth of rests in 4/4 if they come at the start or end of the measure.

If the rests are in the middle of the measure (as shown here in measure 3), two quarter-rest symbols are used instead. This way, the middle of the measure can clearly be seen, making it easier to count the beats. In the final measure, with four beats' rest, we use a single whole-rest symbol.

Example 2

 Audio 03-02

In fact, as we'll soon see, a whole rest indicates an entire measure of silence in any time signature.

Exercises

Clap the following exercises, as before. You'll see that all the note and rest symbols add up to a total of four beats.

Count steadily and be sure to include rests at the beginning of the measure. As before, the tempos are varied, with a one-measure count before each exercise. Take special care where rest symbols are combined.

 Audio 03-ex-01 to 03-ex-07

1. ♩ = 80

2. ♩ = 120

3. ♩ = 100

4. ♩ = 60

5. ♩ = 110

6. ♩ = 100

7. ♩ = 70

CHAPTER 4:
EIGHTH NOTES AND EIGHTH RESTS

This new symbol allows us to split the quarter-note beat into two halves and is known as the *eighth note*. The technical term for splitting the beat into two or more equal parts is *subdividing*. Two eighth notes make up one quarter note. In other words, when the quarter note gets the beat, an eighth note is worth half a beat.

Part 1: The Eighth Note

Sometimes, these half-a-beat symbols appear on their own, with a *flag* added to the quarter-note stem.

When two or more eighth notes are shown together, they're generally joined up with a horizontal *beam*.

Try counting half beats by saying, "one-and-two-and-three-and-four-and." The "and" is the second half of each beat. Each number is **on the beat**, while each "and" is **off the beat**. In other words, the first eighth note takes place at the start of the beat, with the second eighth note coming halfway through. You'll hear a measure of clicks at 60 bpm before the rhythm begins.

Example 1

 Audio 04-01

You'll notice that the beam joins eighth notes in groups of four within in a single measure (not in groups of eight). This is just to make it easier to count.

Some people find it useful to think of pairs of eighth notes together by saying, "coffee." Quarter notes could be "tea."

Example 2

 Audio 04-02

There are lots of variations on this idea. Feel free to find your own words to help you count the beats and their subdivisions.

Exercises

Try clapping through these combinations of half notes, quarter notes, and eighth notes. Keep a steady beat and count confidently. As always, there is a four-beat count before each exercise.

 Audio 04-ex-01 to 04-ex-07

1. ♩ = 60

1 & 2 & 3 & 4 &   1 & 2 & 3 & 4 &   1 & 2 & 3 & 4 &   1 & 2 & 3 & 4 &

2. ♩ = 90

3. ♩ = 110

4. ♩ = 80

5. ♩ = 100

6. ♩ = 60

7. ♩ = 120

Part 2: The Eighth Rest

Just like the whole note, half note, and quarter note, the eighth note also has an equivalent rest symbol.

Here are some individual eighth notes interspersed with eighth rests, with the beat count below. Notice how adjacent eighth notes are only beamed together if the pair begins **on** the beat. Ultimately, this helps you to look ahead and pick up the rhythm more easily as you go.

Let's try this example at two different tempos. Count the beats out loud, including the "ands." Firstly, at the slower 60 bpm.

Example 3

 Audio 04-03

Once you're able to play it smoothly at 60 bpm, let's move it up to a swifter 100 bpm. Pay careful attention to the one-measure count-in to set your beat.

Example 4

 Audio 04-04

Exercises

This time, our exercises include eighth rests. Try these exercises with your own metronome at a variety of different tempos.

 Audio 04-ex-08 to 04-ex-12

8. ♩ = 70

9. ♩ = 100

10. ♩ = 80

11. ♩ = 110

12. ♩ = 60

Part 3: Writing Quarter Rests Correctly

If a quarter rest spans across the half-measure, it's written as two separate eighth rests.

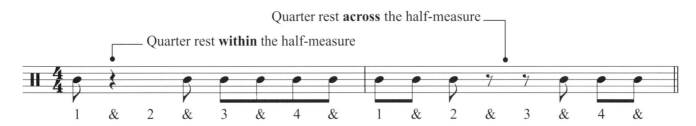

Part 3 Exercises

Let's combine all the half, quarter, and eighth notes and rests we've seen so far.

 Audio 04-ex-13 to 04-ex-19

13. ♩ = 60

1 & 2 & 3 & 4 &   1 & 2 & 3 & 4 &   1 & 2 & 3 & 4 &   1 & 2 & 3 & 4 &

14. ♩ = 90

15. ♩ = 120

16. ♩ = 80

17. ♩ = 60

18. ♩ = 110

19. ♩ = 70

CHAPTER 5: SIMPLE TIME SIGNATURES

We've had a good look at 4/4, which uses the quarter-note symbol as the basic beat. The correct term for a time signature where a quarter note gets the beat is a *simple* time signature. In simple time signatures, the beat naturally has two subdivisions (e.g., a quarter-note beat divides into two eighth notes). Since 4/4 uses four quarter-note beats, it is more precisely known as *simple quadruple time*.

Let's take a peek at another couple of common time signatures that use the quarter-note symbol as the basic beat: 3/4 and 2/4. As they both use a quarter note to represent the beat, these are also called simple time signatures.

3/4: Simple Triple Time

There is a famous type of traditional dance that clearly isn't in 4/4, and it's called the waltz. This has three beats per measure. Try saying 3/4 as, "oom, pah-pah, oom, pah-pah," just like a waltz rhythm.

Example 1

 Audio 05-01

The 3/4 time signature shows three quarter-note beats.

In 3/4, the downbeat (first beat of the measure) is strong and the other two beats are weak.

Here is the eighth-note count for 3/4.

Example 2

 Audio 05-02

3/4 is *simple triple time*. Three beats (triple) that each divide into two eighth notes (simple).

Rests in 3/4

In 3/4, a two-beat rest should be written using separate quarter-rest symbols or, if the rest begins on an off-beat, with a combination of eighth and quarter rests. It will not be written with a half rest. A whole measure's-worth of rest in any time signature is shown with a whole rest.

Example 3

 Audio 05-03

2/4: Simple Duple Time

This two-beat meter is used in march music. It's pretty easy to hear the "left, right" feel of a march rhythm, which always has two beats per measure. You can hear that the first beat is naturally strong and the second beat is weak.

The eighth-note count for 2/4 is easy enough to imagine.

Example 4

 Audio 05-04

2/4 is *simple duple time*. That is two beats (duple), which each divide into two eighth notes (simple).

Exercises

We are going to practice exercises in 2/4, 3/4, and 4/4. Take care to count along with the count-in before you start each exercise. (For the 2/4 and 3/4 exercises, there are **two** measures of count before the rhythm begins.) Doing this will allow you to get a feel for the underlying meter, and that will help you to keep the beats moving steadily on. As a practical musician, it's a good habit to get into.

 Audio 05-ex-01 to 05-ex-14

3.   ♩ = 110

4.   ♩ = 80

5.   ♩ = 90

6.   ♩ = 110

7.   ♩ = 80

8.   ♩ = 60

9.   ♩ = 90

10. ♩ = 100

11. ♩ = 60

12. ♩ = 70

13. ♩ = 120

14. ♩ = 100

CHAPTER 6: 16TH NOTES

Now for another subdivision: the 16th note. There are four of these in a quarter note, meaning there will be 16 in a measure of 4/4.

16th notes are drawn just like eighth notes but with two flags.

Like the eighth note, 16th notes can be joined together with beams. 16th notes have two parallel beams.

When four 16th notes are played in the space of a single quarter note, you can join four of them together.

16th rests are drawn just like eighth rests, but with an extra flag.

We'll look at 16th rests more closely in chapter 12 (p. 47).

An easy way to imagine a group of four 16th notes together might be to say, "cup and saucer." One "cup and saucer" takes the same time as one "tea" or one "coffee." Take a listen to the audio track to hear this in action!

Example 1

 Audio 06-01

The standard way of counting 16th notes is like this. You'll remember we counted eighth notes with "one-and-two-and-three-and-four-and." Well, for 16th notes, we write "e" (spoken as "ee") and "a" (spoken as "ah") in-between, making four syllables for each beat. In this way, you would say, "one-e-and-a, two-e-and-a" and so on. These are known as the *count syllables*.

Example 2

Audio 06-02

You can combine eighth notes and 16th notes within a single quarter-note beat, too. Here are the various possible groupings. Notice that the notes within a single quarter-note count are beamed together with either a single beam (eighth noets) or two beams (16th notes). Take a close look at beat 3, where the 16th notes are separated by an eighth note, and you'll see how the 16th-note beams are detached from one another.

Example 3

Audio 06-03

These groupings of 16th notes and eighth notes are very common. Soon, you'll be able to recognize the different combinations of beat-groupings and know immediately how they should sound together.

Exercises

Let's look at some exercises that include 16th-note rhythms. Clapping starts to get more challenging as the notes are closer together. You might find it easier to say the rhythms, either using the count syllables or any other sound you like; or else tap the rhythms out with your hands on your lap or on a tabletop.

To give you a chance to count and clap clearly, the tempos are slower for 16th-note exercises. Slower tempos have their own challenges, though. The slower you play, the longer the mistakes last, so it's important to play precisely!

Audio 06-ex-01 to 06-ex-07

3.　♩ = 70

4.　♩ = 60

5.　♩ = 80

6.　♩ = 40

7.　♩ = 60

CHAPTER 7: EXTENDED NOTES

It's time to look at some ways we can extend the duration of a note. The first common way to increase the length of a note is by adding a dot.

Dotted Notes

Adding a dot to a note symbol increases the duration by half. In this first example, a quarter note in 4/4 has a dot added to it. It becomes a *dotted quarter note*, worth a combined value of one and a half beats—one beat for the quarter note and another half for the dot. Look at the beat count. It extends to the full duration of the note before the silent counts take over.

Example 1

 **Audio 07-01**

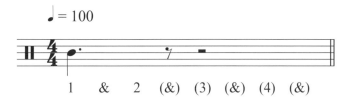

Half notes can be dotted, too.

Example 2

 **Audio 07-02**

Indeed, any note value can have a dot added as long as there's room in the measure. Dotted eighth notes are often paired with the "left over" portion of the beat, which is a 16th note. You'll soon learn to spot this pair of notes and instantly understand the rhythm. As ever, accurate counting is the key here.

Notice how the 16th notes are shown with a detached, extra beam. Try to say the in-between beat counts (in this case the second and third 16th note) under your breath so you get a real feel for the way the beat subdivides.

Example 3

 **Audio 07-03**

It'll help if you try playing this kind of exercise at different tempos, too. Using a metronome or going freehand, try to feel that the beat is split into four equal quarters, with the final 16th note in each pairing coming right on that fourth quarter of the beat.

The "other" arrangement of this pairing—putting the 16th note before the dotted eighth note—isn't quite as common, but you're sure to come across it from time to time. Again, count all four subdivisions, since this will help you to play the next beat on time.

Example 4

 Audio 07-04

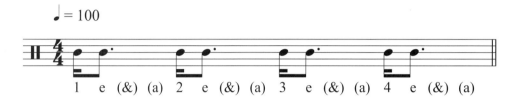

Dotted Rests

You can even add dots to rests! Take a look at these examples. Firstly, a dotted quarter rest combining a quarter rest and an eighth rest together. Secondly, a dotted eighth rest made up of an eighth rest and a 16th rest added together.

Ties

The other way to extend note values is by joining two symbols together with a bowed line called a tie. There are a couple of reasons to do this. Firstly, if you want a note to go across a bar line you need to use two separate symbols and join them up with a tie, as shown in the following example.

In this example, the last note of the first measure actually lasts for two beats, so it's the equivalent of a half note. We can't write a half note at that point because we only have a single beat of the measure remaining. By using a tie, the note continues over the bar line and ends after the first beat of the following measure.

Example 5

 Audio 07-05

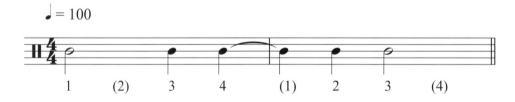

This next example shows how a very long note might look. We're in 3/4 and the single note value that takes up a whole measure is a dotted half note. A dotted half note is worth three quarter-note beats. The addition of ties creates a single note that lasts for four measures. In 4/4, you would likewise extend whole notes by tying them together, and in 2/4 you would do the same with half notes.

Example 6

 Audio 07-06

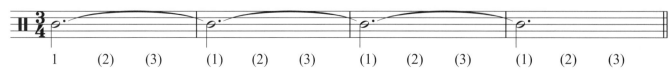

Exercises

These exercises introduce dotted notes and ties. There are no rests, so you'll always be playing a note! Subdivide each beat and count until you are sure how all of the notes fit together. Take it slowly until it feels right. The exercises will become progressively more challenging.

Take particular care over tied or dotted notes that begin on an off-beat, because it's not always so obvious when they finish. These notes create off-beat accents that displace the natural meter of the time signature, making it easier to lose track of the beat. We'll look more closely at this sort of thing in Chapter 11 (p. 43).

 Audio 07-ex-01 to 07-ex-08

1. ♩ = 100

2. ♩ = 60

3. ♩ = 90

4. ♩ = 70

5. ♩ = 90

6. ♩ = 60

7. ♩ = 50

8. ♩ = 100

Here are some with various rests, too. Give yourself a couple of meaures to set the meter before you start each one. Careful counting is the key!

 Audio 07-ex-09 to 07-ex-16

9.　♩ = 60

1 & 2 & 3 & 4 &　1 & 2 & 3　& 4 &　1 & 2 & 3 & 4 &　1 & 2 & 3 & 4 &

10.　♩ = 80

11.　♩ = 70

12.　♩ = 60

13.　♩ = 100

14.　♩ = 60

15.　♩ = 80

16.　♩ = 90

CHAPTER 8: COMPOUND TIME SIGNATURES

In *compound* time signatures, the beat subdivides into three equal parts. The same rhythm symbols are used as in a simple time signature, but now they're arranged a bit differently.

In the simple time signatures we have encountered, the quarter note gets the beat. In compound time signatures, the beat is represented by a dotted quarter note. If you're used to thinking of a beat and a quarter note as the same thing, then it might take a moment for you to adjust to this idea. But as soon as you see it in action, it'll make perfect sense.

6/8: Compound Duple Time

The most common example of a compound time signature is 6/8. The count for these groups of three is, "one-and-ah, two-and-ah."

By the way, we're used to seeing a quarter-note bpm for the metronome marking, whereas now we'll be using a dotted quarter note instead.

As always, say the beat count out loud as you listen to the audio example.

Example 1

 Audio 08-01

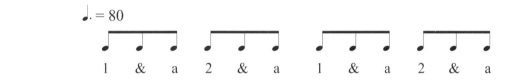

There are two beats in each measure, now shown as dotted quarter notes. Each dotted quarter note is worth one quarter note, plus a half. In other words, each dotted quarter note equals three eighth notes. This means we have two beats per measure, with each beat subdivided into three.

The correct term for this is *compound duple time*. (Compound for the way the beats subdivide into three, and duple for the total number of beats per measure.)

Most pieces that use 6/8 have a dance-like feel. Compare a measure of eighth notes in 6/8 to a measure of eighth notes in 3/4. They both contain a total of six eighth notes, but they're grouped differently. This is shown by the beaming and felt by the counting.

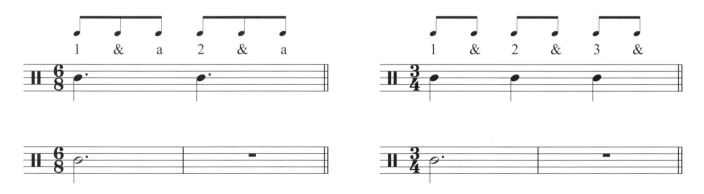

For a note that occupies an entire measure of 6/8, we use the dotted minim (as we do for 3/4). Similarly, an entire measure's rest is indicated by a whole rest.

9/8: Compound Triple Time

In 9/8, there are three beats per measure. This is known as *compound triple time*. Again, be sure to say the beat count as you listen to the audio.

Example 2

 Audio 08-02

For a note that occupies an entire measure of 9/8, we now need to use two symbols—a dotted half note and a dotted quarter note—tied together. As before, an entire measure's rest is indicated by a whole rest.

12/8: Compound Quadruple Time

As you can imagine, this same idea of subdividing the beats into three can be applied to a four-beat meter, too. This gives us 12/8, or *compound quadruple time*. Say the beat count as you listen to the audio and hear the four clear beats in the measure.

Example 3

 Audio 08-03

A single dotted whole note fills a measure of 12/8. As usual, we use the familiar whole rest to show an entire measure's rest.

Exercises

Here are some rhythm exercises in compound time signatures.

 Audio 08-ex-01 to 08-ex-07

1. ♩. = 60

2. ♩. = 50

3. ♩. = 40

4. ♩. = 70

5. ♩. = 80

6. ♩. = 30

7. ♩. = 60

Let's take it up a notch with the addition of some rests. Remember, a dotted quarter rest is worth a single beat.

Audio 08-ex-08 to 08-ex-14

8.   ♩. = 50

1 & a 2 & a   1 & a 2 & a   1 & a 2 & a   1 & a 2 & a

9.   ♩. = 60

10.   ♩. = 40

11.   ♩. = 60

12.   ♩. = 60

13.   ♩. = 40

14.   ♩. = 60

In this next group of exercises, we'll add some ties and faster tempos, so listen carefully to the count-in. Watch out for eighth notes that start on an "and" or an "ah" and are tied to the following note!

Audio 08-ex-15 to 08-ex-21

15. ♩. = 70

1 & a 2 & a 1 & a 2 & a 1 & a 2 & a 1 & a 2 & a

16. ♩. = 80

17. ♩. = 50

18. ♩. = 70

19. ♩. = 60

20. ♩. = 50

21. ♩. = 90

CHAPTER 9: TRIPLETS

As we've seen, simple time signatures all have a basic beat that subdivides into two. In 4/4, for example, the quarter-note beat subdivides into two eighth notes. Those eighth notes can be subdivided further, into two 16th notes each.

Example 1

 Audio 09-01

It is also possible to subdivide this quarter-note beat into three. This is where *triplets* come in. Triplets are groups of **three** notes played in the space of **two**.

Look at the following rhythm. In this example, the third beat in each measure contains three eighth notes, rather than two. Together, they equal the length of two standard eighth notes. The triplet eighth notes are grouped by a single beam, with an additional "3" to indicate the triplet.

The triplets are played evenly but usually with an accent on the first triplet eighth note of the group. Clap and count, taking care to say the beat counts on the third beat without rushing.

Example 2

 Audio 09-02

We can also create quarter-note triplets, with three notes played in the space of two beats. The three quarter-note triplets in this next example take the place of two ordinary quarter notes. Bear in mind that you won't be playing a note right on beat 4, so it makes more sense to count "three-and-a" right across the two-beat duration of the triplet.

Clap them clearly and evenly. Listen out for the way the quarter-note triplet is played **against** the fourth beat. As always, count out loud as you clap. It might not feel very natural at first, but you'll soon recognize the pattern.

Example 3

 Audio 09-03

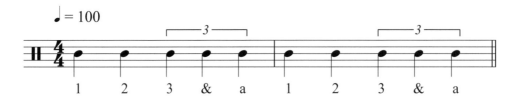

You can even include rests within triplets. Try this rhythm, which is the same as Example 2 but with the middle note of each triplet group replaced by a rest. You'll need to count the triplets carefully, including the "missing" one.

Example 4

 Audio 09-04

In fact, it's possible to combine different note values within a single triplet. In the next example, the first two eighth notes in a group of triplet eighth notes (left) make up the value of a triplet quarter note (right).

Example 5

 Audio 09-05

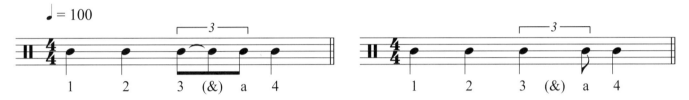

Exercises

These exercises contain various triplets with a few rests. There are one or two sneaky surprises, too! It might help if you begin by clapping or tapping quarter- and eighth-note triplets to a metronome until you feel them more instinctively.

 Audio 09-ex-01 to 09-ex-14

11. ♩ = 60

12. ♩ = 110

13. ♩ = 70

14. ♩ = 90

CHAPTER 10:
MORE SIMPLE TIME SIGNATURES

It is time to examine a few more simple time signatures. Remember, a simple time signature has a beat that naturally divides into two. Here are some time signatures in which the half note gets the beat (indicated by "2" as the bottom number in the time signature).

2/2: Simple Duple Time

2/2 contains two half-note beats per measure. It uses the same symbols as 4/4, and rhythms in 2/2 even look identical to those in 4/4. So, why do we even use 2/2?

As you can see below, both examples contain a measure comprising four quarter notes. The main difference is that 2/2 has two strong beats per measure, with a count of "one-two."

Example 1

Audio 10-01

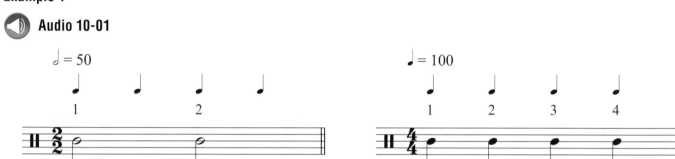

2/2 is generally used for music at a brisk tempo, such as marches, musical theatre, or fast orchestral music. You won't often find it in pop and rock, and as far as writing rhythms out or clapping them, there's nothing at all to tell it apart from 4/4. In the above example, the metronome markings show that a quarter note has the same duration in both time signatures.

You might remember that 4/4 is sometimes referred to as common time, with a symbol like a C replacing the numbers in the time signature. 2/2 can also be known as *cut common time*, represented with a C dissected by a vertical line (below). You'll even occasionally see 2/2 referred to as *alla breve*.

Often, a 2/2 time signature is used to simplify the notation. In the next example, if the 2/2 rhythm were played at twice the tempo of the 4/4 rhythm, they would sound identical. But the note symbols used in 2/2 are much easier to read for a musician than the equivalents in 4/4.

The metronome markings show that the half-note beats in the first rhythm are at the same speed as the quarter-note beats in the second rhythm.

Example 2

 Audio 10-02

3/2: Simple Triple Time

The half note can also be used to represent the beat in triple time, with the time signature of 3/2. Music with this time signature is often played at a swift tempo and with three rather evenly stressed beats. Here, a note lasting an entire measure is written as a dotted whole note.

As with the time signatures we've already seen, an entire measure of silence is indicated by a whole rest.

Example 3

 Audio 10-03

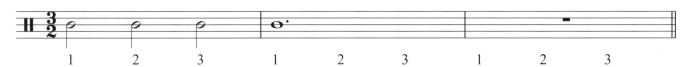

4/2: Simple Quadruple Time

A 4/2 measure is made from four half notes. The note lasting en entire measure is a rhythm symbol we haven't seen before now. It is called a *double whole note*. Representing a duration of twice the length of a whole note, the double whole note also has its own rest symbol, which you'll need for an entire measure's rest in 4/2.

Just like in 4/4, you'll count four beats but with half notes rather than quarter notes. Here is a measure of half notes, together with a double whole note and a double whole rest in action.

Example 4

 Audio 10-04

3/8: Simple Triple Time

Our final time signature has an eighth note as the basic beat. 3/8 has just three eighth notes and is traditionally used for lively dances with three beats per measure. The most obvious difference between 3/8 and 3/4 is in the rhythm symbols used.

Notice below that consecutive eighth notes are beamed in groups of three and that a quarter rest is shown as two separate eighth rests. This helps with counting. An entire measure's rest is the familiar whole rest.

In this example, the metronome marking indicates an eighth note as the basic beat.

Example 5

 Audio 10-05

The Beat Count

The beat count for time signatures that use the half note as the beat follows the same method, whether you are reading music in 2/2, 3/2, or 4/2. Here is this beat-count method, applied to 2/2.

And here is the subdivided beat count for 3/8.

Exercises

Clap and count these exercises, but beware the tempos! 3/8 isn't necessarily four times faster than 3/2.

  Audio 10-ex-01 to 10-ex-08

1.   ♩ = 60

1 & a 2 & 1 & a 2 e & a 1 e & 2 & a 1 & a 2 &

2.   ♩ = 70

3.   ♩ = 100

4.   ♩ = 60

5.   ♩ = 80

6.   ♪ = 140

7.   ♩ = 80

8.   ♪ = 160

And now, with some rests and ties added.

 Audio 10-ex-09 to 10-ex-14

9. $\quad \frac{1}{2} = 60$

1 e & a 2 e & 3 e &   1 e & 2 & 3 e & a

1 e & 2 e & a 3 &   1 e & 2 & 3 &

10. $\quad \flat = 140$

11. $\quad \flat = 50$

12. $\quad \flat = 60$

13. $\quad \flat = 80$

14. $\quad \flat = 140$

CHAPTER 11: SYNCOPATION

The rhythms we've looked at up to this point tend to contain accents that come on the beat. They follow the natural meter of the time signature and the pulse is usually easy to hear.

What Is Syncopation?

Clap through this example, counting aloud, and you'll hear how easy it is to follow. The strong beats—1 and 3—are naturally accented. Where eighth notes appear, they are always in pairs, so that the on-beat eighth notes are stressed.

Example 1

 Audio 11-01

When a rest occurs on a strong beat or when a note extends across the following strong beat, our sense of the natural placement of beats can start to shift. Try the next example, clapping and counting, and hear how accents are now placed on weak beats.

Example 2

 Audio 11-02

This displacement of the strong beat is called *syncopation*. Syncopated rhythms contain accents in unexpected places.

Syncopation is also created by accenting off-beats. In the next example, some of the off-beat notes are followed by a rest or they are extended by dots and ties, creating off-beat accents that go against the underlying pulse. Clap and count as before, and hear how you're now often accenting the "and."

Example 3

 Audio 11-03

Syncopation is an important part of jazz music and related styles such as ragtime. (In fact, ragtime music gets its name from the "ragged" nature of the syncopated rhythms.) But, syncopation can occur in many other styles of music, too.

Reading Rhythms with Syncopation

Reading and playing any rhythm requires careful counting. With syncopation, this is even more so! There are some simple ways to make things easier.

Try reading through the previous example by counting the beat counts written below the notes. Say the beat counts where notes occur out loud, whispering the others under your breath. This is a very common technique for getting to grips with a hard-to-read rhythmic figure, whatever instrument you play. Here's the same example, but this time with the "whispered" counts greyed out.

Listen to the audio to hear how the count might sound. By "speak-and-whisper counting" and accenting in this way, you'll clearly hear the syncopations.

Another helpful technique is to tap steady eighth notes out on your lap or tabletop by alternating your hands. With one hand tapping the on-beats and the other hand tapping the off-beats in constant eighth notes, speak the rhythm over the top.

You should find that you naturally "feel" the off-beat eighth notes matching your off-beat tap. If, for example, you find yourself singing an off-beat eighth note when your on-beat hand is tapping, you'll know it's not right!

Written Accents

Syncopation is also created by playing unexpected accents that are written into the music. The symbol $>$ indicates an accented note.

The next example contains constant eighth notes in 3/4. The second and fourth measures contain an accented off-beat note. Normally, you would play the third eighth note of these measures with a little stress because it's on the beat, but now you'll need to delay the stress until the fourth eighth note.

The effect is as if a measure of 3/4 alternates with a measure of 6/8.

Audio 11-05

Grouping Notes Correctly

Writing out musical notation in the right way can also help to make off-beat rhythms easier to read. Here's an example in 4/4 with continuous off-beat quarter notes.

 **Audio 11-06**

This syncopation is a bit hard to read, especially in the middle of the measure. If we re-write the middle quarter note as a pair of tied eighth notes, we can instantly see where the middle of the measure is. It's the same rhythm but now with the two halves of the measure clearly defined. Once you're used to it, it makes things a lot easier!

Likewise, with off-beat eighth notes. Here's how they would look in two measures of 4/4. As you can see, even with the beat counts written underneath, it's hard to see where you are in the measure.

 **Audio 11-07**

We'd rather write them as pairs of tied 16th notes if they span from the end of one beat to the start of the next.

Exercises

Before attempting to clap through these exercises along with the audio, try using some of the aforementioned techniques, counting slowly. Practice makes perfect, so get used to reading a rhythm over until it makes sense.

 Audio 11-ex-01 to 11-ex-06

1. ♩ = 100

2. ♩ = 90

3. ♩ = 80

4. ♩ = 110

5. ♩ = 100

6. ♩. = 60

CHAPTER 12: 16TH RESTS

Writing Rhythms with 16th Rests

16th rests tend to break up the natural groupings of written notes, making rhythms a challenge to count and play correctly. When it comes to writing them, it's important to group symbols in a logical fashion. Take this example, which is quite confusing even if you count carefully as you clap.

Example 1

 Audio 12-01

Here, the rest symbols break up the natural groupings of the notes themselves and make the rhythms very hard to read.

By joining the beams across the rests, it's easier to spot notes that "belong" together and the individual beats are clearly indicated. Here's the same rhythm, but with the beams written a bit more helpfully. You should find this version easier to follow.

Example 2

 Audio 12-01

Eventually, you'll start to recognize particular combinations and patterns as groups of notes rather than having to think through each individual rhythmic unit. In the meantime, counting is your friend!

16th-Note Rhythm Figures

Here are lots of combinations of 16th notes and eighth notes (together with their rests) that you could find in a single quarter-note beat. Each beat grouping is separated by a dotted line to help you. Try to hear the sound of each individual beat grouping—clap them all through and familiarize yourself with each one. Notice that in a few places, the 16th-note beams run right over the rest symbols.

None of the beat groups here are especially difficult to count or play, but linking them together is much more of a challenge. The beat counts will also help. You could clap the rhythm as you say the beat count out loud or use the speak-and-whisper technique outlined in the previous chapter. Just be patient, take it slowly, and—above all—count!

There are two audio tracks for this example: at 30 bpm and 70 bpm. You'll find that at the slower speed, it's easy to hear the individual notes. At the faster tempo, you're much more likely to hear the groups of notes together as rhythmic phrases.

Example 3

 Audio 12-02 and 12-03

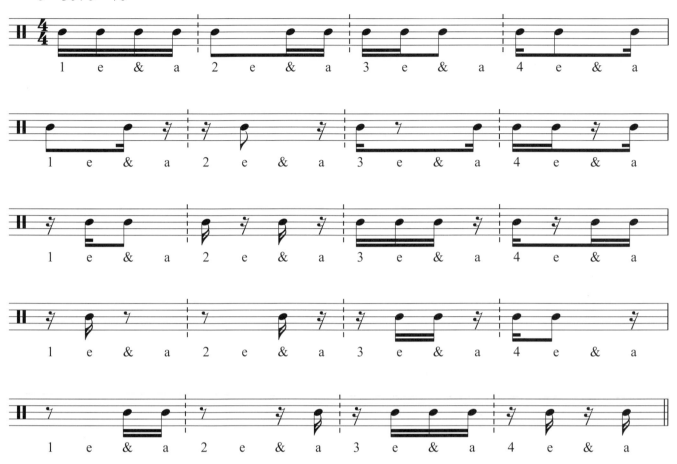

Try jumping from one group to the next; mix up the order, take pauses, try them at different tempos, and maybe even play them on different instruments. It will feel quite different to clap them, sing them, bang them out on a drum, or play them on the piano, for example.

Exercises

Here are some rhythms that include 16th rests among various other note values. Tapping, rather than clapping, will probably be easier with these shorter note values.

You might find it useful to break the more complex rhythms down into combinations that make up a single beat and familiarize yourself with these groupings a little before attempting the exercises. Some of the exercises have rhythms beamed across the rests, but not all of them!

 Audio 12-ex-01 to 12-ex-09

2. ♩. = 50

3. ♩ = 60

4. ♩ = 65

5. ♩ = 75

6. ♩ = 60

7. ♩. = 50

8. ♩ = 75

9. ♩ = 65

CHAPTER 13: 32ND NOTES

There's one more subdivision to look at: the 32nd note. As you can imagine, this is half the duration of a 16th note.

32nd notes are drawn like 16th notes but with an additional flag.

When 32nd notes are beamed together, they have triple beams. They are grouped together like this to make them easier to read.

With eight 32nd notes to a quarter-note beat, there are 32 in a single measure of 4/4.

32nd rests are drawn just like 16th rests but with an additional flag.

Tapping 32nd Notes

To get a feel for 32nd notes, tap through the next exercise in the following way.

- At a slow tempo (the recording is at 40 bpm), tap even quarter notes in 4/4 with one finger.

- After two measures, you'll need to tap eighth notes. Use the same single finger and give a light accent to the on-beat eighth notes.

- After two measures of eighth notes, you're playing 16th notes, and if you relax you'll still be able to play them all with the same finger. Remember to accent the on-beat 16th notes.

- Finally, you'll need to bring the opposite hand into play for the 32nd notes.

Tapping rhythms is a bit of a knack, but it's a useful tool; drummers and percussionists often tap out rhythms this way. Focussing on which hand you're using for the different subdivisions (drummers call this "sticking") will help you tap out fast notes reliably and confidently.

Example 1

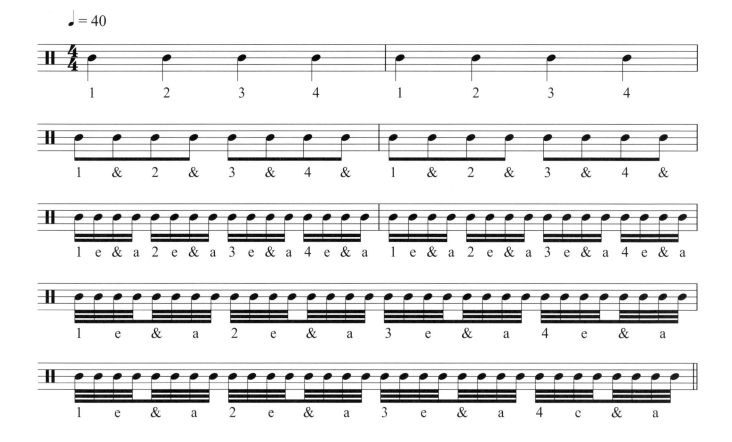

Repeated 32nd Notes

As you can see above, when several 32nd notes are played together, the music can soon look a bit crowded. If they are all at the same pitch, you'll sometimes see repeated 32nd notes written using an abbreviation, like the example below. Here's a whole 4/4 measure of 32nd notes. The first quarter-note beat is written out in full—that's eight 32nd notes—but the following beats are written as quarter notes with 32nd-note *tremolo strokes*, drawn as three beams just like a 32nd note.

Example 2

Exercises

With 32nd notes, tapping and clapping is only really possible at slower tempos, so that's what we have here. You'll need to focus—not only to play the fast notes accurately, but to play the longer notes precisely, too.

 Audio 13-ex-01 to 13-ex-07

Bonus Tracks

Just for fun, here are a number of sample audio tracks with music in different time signatures. Hopefully, these will give you an idea of the character of each time signature, making it easier for you to feel the beat and recognize common rhythmic groupings within each one.

🔊 **Sample Music: 4/4**

🔊 **Sample Music: 6/8**

🔊 **Sample Music: 3/4**

🔊 **Sample Music: 12/8**

🔊 **Sample Music: 2/4**

JAZZ INSTRUCTION & IMPROVISATION

BOOKS FOR ALL INSTRUMENTS FROM HAL LEONARD

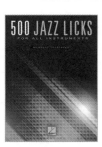

500 JAZZ LICKS
by Brent Vaartstra

This book aims to assist you on your journey to play jazz fluently. These short phrases and ideas we call "licks" will help you understand how to navigate the common chords and chord progressions you will encounter. Adding this vocabulary to your arsenal will send you down the right path and improve your jazz playing, regardless of your instrument.
00142384 ....$16.99

1001 JAZZ LICKS
by Jack Shneidman
Cherry Lane Music

This book presents 1,001 melodic gems played over dozens of the most important chord progressions heard in jazz. This is the ideal book for beginners seeking a well-organized, easy-to-follow encyclopedia of jazz vocabulary, as well as professionals who want to take their knowledge of the jazz language to new heights.
02500133 ....$14.99

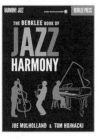

THE BERKLEE BOOK OF JAZZ HARMONY
by Joe Mulholland & Tom Hojnacki

Learn jazz harmony, as taught at Berklee College of Music. This text provides a strong foundation in harmonic principles, supporting further study in jazz composition, arranging, and improvisation. It covers basic chord types and their tensions, with practical demonstrations of how they are used in characteristic jazz contexts and an accompanying recording that lets you hear how they can be applied.
00113755 Book/Online Audio.....................$19.99

BUILDING A JAZZ VOCABULARY
By Mike Steinel

A valuable resource for learning the basics of jazz from Mike Steinel of the University of North Texas. It covers: the basics of jazz • how to build effective solos • a comprehensive practice routine • and a jazz vocabulary of the masters.
00849911 ....$19.99

COMPREHENSIVE TECHNIQUE FOR JAZZ MUSICIANS
2ND EDITION
by Bert Ligon
Houston Publishing

An incredible presentation of the most practical exercises an aspiring jazz student could want. All are logically interwoven with fine "real world" examples from jazz to classical. This book is an essential anthology of technical, compositional, and theoretical exercises, with lots of musical examples.
00030455 ....$34.99

EAR TRAINING
by Keith Wyatt,
Carl Schroeder and Joe Elliott
Musicians Institute Press

Covers: basic pitch matching • singing major and minor scales • identifying intervals • transcribing melodies and rhythm • identifying chords and progressions • seventh chords and the blues • modal interchange, chromaticism, modulation • and more.
00695198 Book/Online Audio.....................$24.99

EXERCISES AND ETUDES FOR THE JAZZ INSTRUMENTALIST
by J.J. Johnson

Designed as study material and playable by any instrument, these pieces run the gamut of the jazz experience, featuring common and uncommon time signatures and keys, and styles from ballads to funk. They are progressively graded so that both beginners and professionals will be challenged by the demands of this wonderful music.
00842018 Bass Clef Edition $19.99
00842042 Treble Clef Edition $16.95

HOW TO PLAY FROM A REAL BOOK
by Robert Rawlins

Explore, understand, and perform the songs in real books with the techniques in this book. Learn how to analyze the form and harmonic structure, insert an introduction, interpret the melody, improvise on the chords, construct bass lines, voice the chords, add substitutions, and more. It addresses many aspects of solo and small band performance that can improve your own playing and your understanding of what others are doing around you.
00312097 ....$19.99

JAZZ DUETS
ETUDES FOR PHRASING AND ARTICULATION
by Richard Lowell
Berklee Press

With these 27 duets in jazz and jazz-influenced styles, you will learn how to improve your ear, sense of timing, phrasing, and your facility in bringing theoretical principles into musical expression. Covers: jazz staccato & legato • scales, modes & harmonies • phrasing within and between measures • swing feel • and more.
00302151 ....$14.99

JAZZ THEORY & WORKBOOK
by Lilian Dericq &
Étienne Guéreau

Designed for all instrumentalists, this book teaches how jazz standards are constructed. It is also a great resource for arrangers and composers seeking new writing tools. While some of the musical examples are pianistic, this book is not exclusively for keyboard players.
00159022 ....$19.99

JAZZ THEORY RESOURCES
by Bert Ligon
Houston Publishing, Inc.

This is a jazz theory text in two volumes. **Volume 1 includes**: review of basic theory • rhythm in jazz performance • triadic generalization • diatonic harmonic progressions and analysis • substitutions and turnarounds • and more. **Volume 2 includes**: modes and modal frameworks • quartal harmony • extended tertian structures and triadic superimposition • pentatonic applications • coloring "outside" the lines and beyond • and more.
00030458 Volume 1 ....$39.99
00030459 Volume 2 ....$32.99

JAZZOLOGY
THE ENCYCLOPEDIA OF JAZZ THEORY FOR ALL MUSICIANS
by Robert Rawlins and
Nor Eddine Bahha

This comprehensive resource covers a variety of jazz topics, for beginners and pros of any instrument. The book serves as an encyclopedia for reference, a thorough methodology for the student, and a workbook for the classroom.
00311167 ....$24.99

MODALOGY
SCALES, MODES & CHORDS: THE PRIMORDIAL BUILDING BLOCKS OF MUSIC
by Jeff Brent with Schell Barkley

Primarily a music theory reference, this book presents a unique perspective on the origins, interlocking aspects, and usage of the most common scales and modes in occidental music. Anyone wishing to seriously explore the realms of scales, modes, and their real-world functions will find the most important issues dealt with in meticulous detail within these pages.
00312274 ....$24.99

THE SOURCE
THE DICTIONARY OF CONTEMPORARY AND TRADITIONAL SCALES
by Steve Barta

This book serves as an informative guide for people who are looking for good, solid information regarding scales, chords, and how they work together. It provides right and left hand fingerings for scales, chords, and complete inversions. Includes over 20 different scales, each written in all 12 keys.
00240885 ....$19.99

HAL•LEONARD®
www.halleonard.com

Prices, contents & availability subject to change without notice.

0421
068

JAZZ INSTRUCTION & IMPROVISATION

BOOKS FOR ALL INSTRUMENTS FROM HAL LEONARD

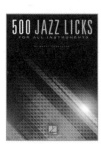

500 JAZZ LICKS
by Brent Vaartstra
This book aims to assist you on your journey to play jazz fluently. These short phrases and ideas we call "licks" will help you understand how to navigate the common chords and chord progressions you will encounter. Adding this vocabulary to your arsenal will send you down the right path and improve your jazz playing, regardless of your instrument.
00142384 ....$16.99

1001 JAZZ LICKS
by Jack Shneidman
Cherry Lane Music
This book presents 1,001 melodic gems played over dozens of the most important chord progressions heard in jazz. This is the ideal book for beginners seeking a well-organized, easy-to-follow encyclopedia of jazz vocabulary, as well as professionals who want to take their knowledge of the jazz language to new heights.
02500133 ....$17.99

THE BERKLEE BOOK OF JAZZ HARMONY
by Joe Mulholland & Tom Hojnacki
Learn jazz harmony, as taught at Berklee College of Music. This text provides a strong foundation in harmonic principles, supporting further study in jazz composition, arranging, and improvisation. It covers basic chord types and their tensions, with practical demonstrations of how they are used in characteristic jazz contexts and an accompanying recording that lets you hear how they can be applied.
00113755 Book/Online Audio..................$29.99

BUILDING A JAZZ VOCABULARY
By Mike Steinel
A valuable resource for learning the basics of jazz from Mike Steinel of the University of North Texas. It covers: the basics of jazz • how to build effective solos • a comprehensive practice routine • and a jazz vocabulary of the masters.
00849911 ....$22.99

COMPREHENSIVE TECHNIQUE FOR JAZZ MUSICIANS
2ND EDITION
by Bert Ligon
Houston Publishing
An incredible presentation of the most practical exercises an aspiring jazz student could want. All are logically interwoven with fine "real world" examples from jazz to classical. This book is an essential anthology of technical, compositional, and theoretical exercises, with lots of musical examples.
00030455 ....$34.99

EAR TRAINING
by Keith Wyatt,
Carl Schroeder and Joe Elliott
Musicians Institute Press
Covers: basic pitch matching • singing major and minor scales • identifying intervals • transcribing melodies and rhythm • identifying chords and progressions • seventh chords and the blues • modal interchange, chromaticism, modulation • and more.
00695198 Book/Online Audio..................$29.99

EXERCISES AND ETUDES FOR THE JAZZ INSTRUMENTALIST
by J.J. Johnson
Designed as study material and playable by any instrument, these pieces run the gamut of the jazz experience, featuring common and uncommon time signatures and keys, and styles from ballads to funk. They are progressively graded so that both beginners and professionals will be challenged by the demands of this wonderful music.
00842018 Bass Clef Edition..................$22.99
00842042 Treble Clef Edition..................$16.95

HOW TO PLAY FROM A REAL BOOK
by Robert Rawlins
Explore, understand, and perform the songs in real books with the techniques in this book. Learn how to analyze the form and harmonic structure, insert an introduction, interpret the melody, improvise on the chords, construct bass lines, voice the chords, add substitutions, and more. It addresses many aspects of solo and small band performance that can improve your own playing and your understanding of what others are doing around you.
00312097 ....$19.99

JAZZ DUETS
ETUDES FOR PHRASING AND ARTICULATION
by Richard Lowell
Berklee Press
With these 27 duets in jazz and jazz-influenced styles, you will learn how to improve your ear, sense of timing, phrasing, and your facility in bringing theoretical principles into musical expression. Covers: jazz staccato & legato • scales, modes & harmonies • phrasing within and between measures • swing feel • and more.
00302151 ....$14.99

JAZZ THEORY & WORKBOOK
by Lilian Dericq &
Étienne Guéreau
Designed for all instrumentalists, this book teaches how jazz standards are constructed. It is also a great resource for arrangers and composers seeking new writing tools. While some of the musical examples are pianistic, this book is not exclusively for keyboard players.
00159022 ....$19.99

JAZZ THEORY RESOURCES
by Bert Ligon
Houston Publishing, Inc.
This is a jazz theory text in two volumes. **Volume 1 includes**: review of basic theory • rhythm in jazz performance • triadic generalization • diatonic harmonic progressions and analysis • substitutions and turnarounds • and more.
Volume 2 includes: modes and modal frameworks • quartal harmony • extended tertian structures and triadic superimposition • pentatonic applications • coloring "outside" the lines and beyond • and more.
00030458 Volume 1 ....$39.99
00030459 Volume 2 ....$32.99

JAZZOLOGY
THE ENCYCLOPEDIA OF JAZZ THEORY FOR ALL MUSICIANS
by Robert Rawlins and
Nor Eddine Bahha
This comprehensive resource covers a variety of jazz topics, for beginners and pros of any instrument. The book serves as an encyclopedia for reference, a thorough methodology for the student, and a workbook for the classroom.
00311167 ....$24.99

MODALOGY
SCALES, MODES & CHORDS: THE PRIMORDIAL BUILDING BLOCKS OF MUSIC
by Jeff Brent with Schell Barkley
Primarily a music theory reference, this book presents a unique perspective on the origins, interlocking aspects, and usage of the most common scales and modes in occidental music. Anyone wishing to seriously explore the realms of scales, modes, and their real-world functions will find the most important issues dealt with in meticulous detail within these pages.
00312274 ....$24.99

THE SOURCE
THE DICTIONARY OF CONTEMPORARY AND TRADITIONAL SCALES
by Steve Barta
This book serves as an informative guide for people who are looking for good, solid information regarding scales, chords, and how they work together. It provides right and left hand fingerings for scales, chords, and complete inversions. Includes over 20 different scales, each written in all 12 keys.
00240885 ....$19.99

HAL•LEONARD®
www.halleonard.com